INUYASHA

◆ A half-demon with a dog demon father and human mother. Moroha's father.

KAGOME

◆ After graduating high school, she returned to the feudal era to marry and live with Inuyasha. Moroha's mother.

SESSHOMARU

◆ Inuyasha's elder half-brother, whose mother was also a demon. Prideful and sometimes heartless. Towa and Setsuna's father.

RIN

◆ The young human woman who accompanied Sesshomaru on his travels and later married him. Towa and Setsuna's mother.

THE JOURNEY THUS FAR...

Towa is a not-so-ordinar o
grew up in present-day Ja Her
intense vibe and steely-e n
outcast. One day, while u a
pesky ghost, she is attacl owa
is about to succumb when her twin sister Setsuna and cousin Moroha appear out of the blue to join the battle.

The three of them return to the feudal era and finish off the demon together. There, Towa learns that her parents disappeared when she was a little girl, and that shortly thereafter she was separated from the other two and transported into the future. Now that the girls are reunited, the Tree of Ages sends the trio west to find their parents and save both their worlds from total annihilation!

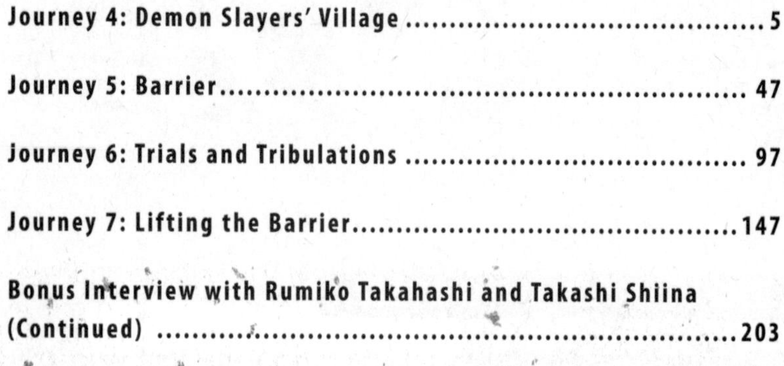
Journey 4: Demon Slayers' Village 5

Journey 5: Barrier 47

Journey 6: Trials and Tribulations 97

Journey 7: Lifting the Barrier 147

Bonus Interview with Rumiko Takahashi and Takashi Shiina (Continued) 203

Journey 4:
Demon Slayers' Village

THDOOM
KRAK KRAK
FLAP
WHOOSH
FLAP
SKWAAAK!!

IT'S TAKING OFF!
DON'T LET IT GET AWAY!!
ZSH
I'LL STOP IT!!
GO, HIRAI-KOTSU!

!!
SLAM
CRASH
ZSHHH
DASH
GOOD!

KRAHHH!!
DO
OM

YEAH
GOT IT!

WOW!
NICE WORK, HISUI!
YEP.
HE DID WELL.

MAYBE HE'LL FILL THE HOLE SETSUNA AND MOROHA LEFT.
HEH... THAT'S A TALL ORDER FOR A MERE HUMAN.
...
TRUE ENOUGH.
SIGH... IF ONLY THEY WERE STILL ON OUR TEAM.

MOM AND POPS HAVE BEEN GONE FOR THREE YEARS, BUSY DOING WHO KNOWS WHAT.
AND MY UNCLE WON'T EVEN TELL ME WHERE SETSUNA AND MOROHA ARE!
GRAB
!!
LOOK OUT! IT'S STILL ALIVE!
FWP
SSH
L
S
!!

GRP
I WARNED YOU TO NEVER LET YOUR GUARD DOWN.
THERE'S NOTHING MORE PERILOUS THAN THE MOMENT AFTER YOU THINK YOU'VE TRIUMPHED.
DEMONS ARE MORE DANGEROUS THAN ORDINARY PREY. THEY STRIKE AT THE **SOUL**.
WHEN YOU FIGHT THEM, YOU MUST NEVER LET UP!!

I'M SORRY, UNCLE.
I MEAN, CHIEF.

HARPIES ARE VERY DANGER-OUS.
WHEN WE WERE TOLD SOMETHING WAS KILLING CATTLE, WE PRESUMED IT WAS A LESSER DEMON.

THAT'S RIGHT.

HARPIES LIVE HIGH IN THE MOUNTAINS, IN PLACES HUMANS DON'T SETTLE.

WE THINK THIS ONE GOT SEPARATED FROM ITS FLOCK.

IT'S BEEN HAPPENING MORE OFTEN LATELY.

WELL, THAT JUST MEANS MORE WORK FOR US SLAYERS!
THAT'S FOR SURE!
I'VE HEARD TELL OF NEW WEAPONS CALLED "GUNS"!
THEY SAY EVEN ORDINARY SAMURAI CAN SINGLEHAND-EDLY TAKE DOWN SMALL MONSTERS WITH THEM!
BWAHAHA

...

WHEN LESSER DEMONS SUDDENLY CHANGE THEIR HABITS...
...IT USUALLY MEANS A MORE POWERFUL DEMON IS ON THE MOVE.
BUT THIS HARPY WAS NO LESSER DEMON.
THIS COULD BE SERIOUS.

DRAT! I WAS HOPING TO IMPRESS MY UNCLE.
KIRARA USUALLY HELPS ME...
...BUT SHE DIDN'T COME ON THE HUNT TODAY.

FLIT
SKUTTLE

POUNCE

AH

IT IS KIRARA!

WHAT ARE YOU DOING WAY OUT HERE?

WHO'S A GOOD GIRL?

HUH?!

IS THAT A... **CAT**?!

ZSH

THAT'S RIGHT, KIRARA! YOUR DOGGIE BIG SIS IS HERE!
PURRRR!
WHAT'S THAT YOU'VE GOT THERE? A LIZARD TAIL?
WHY, THANK YOU! YOU'RE SO KIND! ♪
FLUFF
YOU'RE TAKING IT?
YOU'RE NOT GONNA **EAT** IT, ARE YOU?

SHE'S HAPPY TO SEE YOU TOO, SETSUNA.
HELLO.
YOU'RE LOOKING WELL.

...

...
YES. YES.

SAY HI.
THIS IS TOWA.
PRRRR
SHE'S MY TWIN.

...!
SNIFF
SNIFF
SNIFF
I'VE GOTTA SNUGGLE YOUR FUZZY WUZZY FUR!!
HUF
HUF
YOU'RE SO DARN CUTE!!
!!
FSH
GRRRRWL!!
WHOA!
BOOF

PHEW!
WASN'T EXPECTING THAT...
HYOOOO
WHY DIDN'T YOU TELL ME SHE WAS A DEMON?
ISN'T IT OBVIOUS?
YOU SAID SHE WAS A CAT!
COULDN'T YOU TELL BY HER SCENT?

EVERYTHING IN THIS WORLD SMELLS SUPER-NATURAL.
PLUS, YOU TWO GET YOUR DEMON SCENT ALL OVER EVERY-THING.
THE SMELLS GET ALL MIXED UP.
HEY!
ORDINARY DEMONS STINK! LADIES LIKE US HAVE A SWEET AROMA.

TOWA HAS LIVED TOO LONG IN A WORLD WITHOUT DEMONS.
I HOPE HER INSTINCTS SHARPEN UP QUICKLY.
IT'S AMAZING HERE!
KIRARA IS THE BEST THING I'VE SEEN YET!

I CAN'T BELIEVE SHE CAN CARRY ALL THREE OF US ON HER BACK!
WITH HER ON OUR SIDE, WE'LL REACH THE FAR WEST IN NO TIME!
PURRR
HA HA!
IT'S NOT THAT EASY...

KIRARA IS STRONG AND SWIFT ...
...BUT SHE CAN'T FLY FOR VERY LONG.
WHAT VILLAGE?
RIGHT OVER THERE.
SHE'S JUST TAKING US TO THE VILLAGE NOW.
PRRR...
THE CHIEF'S OUT ON A MISSION?
YOU DIDN'T GO WITH HIM?

OUR DESTINATION TODAY...

...IS THE **DEMON SLAYERS' VILLAGE.**

GRRWR!
I SEE. YOU DON'T WANT THEM TO RELY ON YOU TOO MUCH.
OMIGOSH! IF MY INSTINCTS SHARPEN, WILL I BE ABLE TO TALK TO HER TOO?
NO, ONLY MOROHA CAN DO THAT.
AND I'M PRETTY SURE SHE'S FAKING.

PLLP
FSHHH

!
FWM

THANKS, KIRARA.
YOU'RE A BIG HELP. ♪
AH!
PFFT
SPLASH
MISS...
... SETSU-NA?

I APOLO-GIZE FOR STARTLING YOU.
KIRARA FLEW ME HERE.
HEY! ♪
ME TOO!

JUST A MOMENT!!
DASH
UH...
HUH?

DID WE DO SOMETHING WRONG?
NAH, IT'S NOT THAT.
THEY'RE ALWAYS LIKE THIS.

AS HALF DEMONS, DEMON SLAYING IS OUR CALLING.
WHEN WE WERE OLDER, THIS VILLAGE TOOK US IN.
SO WE KNOW EVERYONE HERE.

THANK YOU FOR WAITING!!
WAP
I APOLO-GIZE FOR MY POOR MANNERS!
WELCOME HOME, MISS SETSUNA!!

PLEASE, MA'AM...
YOU NEEDN'T DRESS UP ON MY ACCOUNT.
BUT I MUST!
I'M IN THE PRESENCE OF THE GREAT MISS SETSUNA!!

KYAAA
KYAAAA

MISS SETSUNA!!
TRMP TRMP TRMP
OH, JOY! MISS SETSUNA'S HERE!!

I'M HERE TOO, YOU KNOW.

AND I'VE BEEN AWAY **LONGER.**

OH YEAH?

WELCOME HOME, KIRARA.

TUP

A WHILE BACK, MOROHA LEFT THE VILLAGE TO HUNT ON HER OWN.

SHE TOOK ON WORK AS A BOUNTY HUNTER.

SHE WOULDN'T EXPLAIN WHY THOUGH.

WE'VE BEEN WORRIED ABOUT HER.

KIN'U! GYOKUTO!
THE SQUIRTS MISSED YOU, MOROHA.
GO SAY HI!
MOROHA!
BIG SIS MOROHA!!

…WHO IS THIS BEAUTIFUL STRANGER?

SHE'S ANDROGYNOUS AND DRESSED AS A WESTERNER AND IT'S ALL STRANGELY THRILLING!

UH …

UM …

HER SHARP EYES ARE AS BRILLIANT AS MISS SETSUNA'S!

THIS IS MY TWIN SISTER. WE WERE SEPARATED TEN YEARS AGO.

HI, I'M TOWA.

UM… THANKS FOR LOOKING AFTER MY TWIN.

SISTERS!!
IT CAN'T BE!!
BLUSH
HER HAND!!
IT'S A DREAM COME TRUE!!
I'M OVERCOME!!

KYAAAA
TOGETHER AGAIN! REUNITED!
OH!
I'M SO GLAD I'M FIT TO BURST!
FSFSFS
THANK YOU, DEITIES!
I MUST DRAW THEM HOLDING HANDS!!
TWO BLAZING SUNS IN MY SKY! WHAT TO DO?!
SORRY ABOUT ALL THIS…
IT'S JUST LIKE MR. KIRIN, MY CLASSICS TEACHER, SAID…
OVER THOUSANDS OF YEARS, THE ONE THING THAT DOESN'T CHANGE IS THE HUMAN HEART.

THE CHIEF HAS RETURNED!!
OPEN THE GATE!!
!
OH NO!
SHOOF
HUH?

AH!
CLOP CLOP
SO THIS IS WHAT THE VILLAGE HAS BEEN CLAMORING ABOUT.

SETSUNA AND MOROHA HAVE RETURNED!
THAT'S RIGHT, CHIEF.
H-HELLO...

SETSUNA
...

ARE YOU TOWA, THEN?
YEAH!

NICE TO MEET YOU, UM...
CHIEF!
CHIEF!

CALL ME KOHAKU.
SO YOU'RE SETSUNA'S TWIN.
YOU HAVE THE SAME EYES.

COOL AND ENTRANCING...
... MUCH LIKE MASTER SESSHOMARU'S.
YOU DON'T THINK THEY'RE SCARY?!
SHINGGG!!

NO ONE'S EVER DESCRIBED MY EYES LIKE THAT BEFORE! I CAN'T BELIEVE IT!
SHH
I DON'T KNOW THE DETAILS, BUT THE CHIEF'S HAD A ROUGH LIFE.
I'M SURE HE'S SEEN WORSE THAN OUR EYES.

I WANT TO HEAR **EVERYTHING.**
HISUI! KIN'U! GYOKUTO!
ESCORT THEM TO THE MANOR.
YOUR PARENTS WILL WANT TO HEAR THEIR STORY TOO, AS WILL MY SISTER AND BROTHER-IN-LAW.
YES, UNCLE!

I'LL BE THERE RIGHT AWAY...
... AFTER I'VE PAID MY RESPECTS.
CLIP
CLOP
HEH HEH ...
BET YOU'RE HAPPY THAT...
... SETSUNA'S BACK, EH, HISUI?
I... H-HAVE NO IDEA WHAT YOU'RE TALKING ABOUT!

UM...
SO...

MAY I GO NOW?
I'VE GOT PLACES TO BE.
NO.
YOU'RE STAYING FOR THIS.
WE CAN GO TO THE CORPSE DEALER LATER.

AND I WANT MY SHARE OF THE BOUNTY FOR THE CROW DEMONS AND THE THREE-EYED CENTIPEDE!
IN FACT, WE OUGHT TO DIVIDE IT THREE WAYS WITH TOWA.
TCH.

?
?
POOR TOWA! YOU LOOK UTTERLY AT SEA!
IF SHE'S FROM LADY KAGOME'S LAND, IT'S NO SURPRISE.

THIS VILLAGE SPECIALIZES IN DEMON SLAYING. IT'S OUR MAIN SOURCE OF INCOME.
IT'S STEADY WORK IN TIMES OF WAR AND PEACE ALIKE.
THESE DAYS, MANY DAIMYO EMPLOY OUR SERVICES.
SOME OF THE MORE NOTORIOUS DEMONS EVEN HAVE BOUNTIES ON THEIR HEADS.
MOROHA HAS BEEN HUNTING THOSE.
IT'S RISKY WORK, BUT THE REWARDS ARE GREAT.

WE USE THE BONES AND HIDES FROM SLAIN DEMONS...
...TO FASHION TOOLS AND CONCOCT MEDICINES.
SLAYERS ARE WELCOME EVERYWHERE.
WE CAN ALSO PICK UP WORK AS SPIES AND MERCENARIES.

DO ALL THOSE GIRLS IN THE VILLAGE...
...COME FROM FAMILIES OF DEMON SLAYERS AND NINJA?
NO...

SOME OF THEM, LIKE MY MOTHER, ARE SLAYERS ...
...BUT PLENTY OF VILLAGERS FARM OR WORK TRADES AND KEEP HOUSE.
MANY OF THE CHILDREN YOU SEE...
...WERE BROUGHT HERE BY MY UNCLE AND MOTHER.

SOME HAVE SPIRIT POWERS AND HAVE COME TO TRAIN.
!
BUT MOST ARE ORPHANS...
... RESCUED FROM WAR OR SLAVERY.

THESE DAYS, THE VILLAGE IS BOOMING.

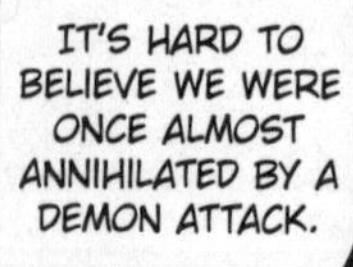
IT'S HARD TO BELIEVE WE WERE ONCE ALMOST ANNIHILATED BY A DEMON ATTACK.

SINCE THEN, WE'VE BEEN GROWING...
... REVIVING OLD SKILLS...
...AND MAKING IT TO WHERE WE ARE TODAY.

FATHER...

FAMILY...

I'VE COME HOME.

I'M LIVING THE LIFE I OWE TO...
...KIKYO, MY SISTER SANGO, KAGURA...
...AND MASTER SESSHOMARU.

THE MEMORIES FROM THAT TIME STILL TWIST INSIDE ME LIKE A KNIFE...
...SO I CLING TO HAPPY MOMENTS.
SO. WHAT'S YOUR NAME?
ME, I'M RIN.
KOHA-KU...
ARE YOU AFRAID OF DYING?
AT LEAST...
...I GOT TO SEE HIM...

MASTER SESSHO-MARU!
SHE ISN'T...
... BREATHING.
THERE IS NOTHING TO GAIN...
...FROM SAVING RIN'S LIFE.
MASTER SESSHO-MARU...
...WAS A PROUD, COLD DEMON WITH EYES THAT BORE THROUGH YOU.
BUT HE LEARNED TO LOVE AND HAVE COMPASSION FOR OTHERS. AND IN THE END HE CHOSE A PATH OF CHANGE.

HE MARRIED RIN, A HUMAN, AND HAD CHILDREN WITH HER.
HUMANS NATURALLY BOND OUT OF LOVE, BUT FOR HIM...
...IT MEANT ALTERING HIS VERY NATURE.

THERE MUST BE A REASON SUCH A PROUD SOUL...
...WOULD WITHDRAW FROM THE WORLD.

I HAVE TO KNOW WHY!
WHATEVER THE COST!

I THOUGHT I'D PREPARED MYSELF...
BUT WILL IT BE ENOUGH?

THE TREE OF AGES BADE YOU GO WEST-WARD TO SAVE THE WORLD.
YOU ASK PERMISSION TO DEPART ON THIS QUEST AND REQUEST A WEAPON FOR TOWA.
IS THAT... ALL?
I'M PREPARED TO PROVIDE YOU WITH A CADRE OF SOLDIERS AND A THOU-SAND LONG GUNS.
NOT TO MENTION MY OWN BODY AND SOUL.
AN ARMY WOULD LEAD TO COLLATERAL DAMAGE.
AND WHAT WOULD WE DO WITH YOUR BODY OR SOUL?
I AGREE. IN THIS POLITICAL CLIMATE, IT'S BETTER TO CROSS THE BORDER...
...WITH AS FEW TROOPS AS POSSIBLE.
BUT YOU MUST TAKE MORE THAN **JUST THE THREE OF YOU!**
IT'S TOO DANGER-OUS.
I'LL GO WITH THEM, UNCLE!
THERE'S NO NEED, HISUI.
THE TRUTH IS...

...YOU'D JUST BE A BURDEN.
SET-SUNA!
BE NICE!
THAT IS TO SAY... WE DON'T NEED YOU...
ER... YOU'D MAKE THINGS MORE DIFFICULT...
THIS IS VERBAL ABUSE!

IS THIS HOW YOU REPAY OUR KINDNESS?!
RAWR!!
"OUR"?
DON'T LOOK AT ME!
HAVE YOU FOR-GOTTEN, HISUI?
THE THREE OF US HAVE DEMON BLOOD IN OUR VEINS.
WE'RE FAR STRONGER THAN WE APPEAR.

WE CAN MAKE SHORT WORK OF DEMONS AND BANDITS. IN FACT, WE WELCOME THE BOUNTIES ATTACHED TO THEM.
IT SAVES US THE TROUBLE OF CARRYING STRINGS OF MON COINS.
NO MERE HUMAN CAN MATCH OUR SPEED OR STRENGTH.
IT'S BETTER FOR US TO TRAVEL ALONE.

WELL... YEAH... BUT...
HMPH.

VERY WELL. DO AS YOU PLEASE.
THOUGH I WISH I COULD OFFER YOU MORE AID.

I APOLOGIZE, CHIEF.

NO, IT WAS SELFISH OF ME TO ATTEMPT TO INVOLVE MYSELF.
DON'T WORRY ABOUT IT.

I ONLY WISH TO RE-PAY MY DEBTS...
...TO MAKE AMENDS FOR MY PAST.
MY HEART IS A HUNGRY CHILD, STARVED FOR REDEMPTION.

EVEN THOUGH I KNOW NOTHING I DO WILL BE ENOUGH.

UM... CHIEF?
KO-HAKU?
YOU TALKED LIKE YOU KNEW OUR DAD REALLY WELL...
HE'S A DEMON, RIGHT?

WHAT OF IT?
I DON'T KNOW WHAT IT MEANS TO BE THE DAUGHTER OF A DEMON.

WHEN YOU MEET HIM, YOU WILL FIND OUT FOR YOUR-SELF.
THAT'S WHY YOU'VE EMBARKED ON THIS JOURNEY, ISN'T IT?
FOR NOW...
...BE PROUD OF WHO YOU ARE.

OF YOUR POWER.
OF YOUR EYES.
YOU INHER-ITED THEM FROM MASTER SESSHOMARU, AND YOU SHOULDN'T HIDE THEM.
!

YOU TOO, MOROHA.
HUH?
YOU RECEIVED GREAT GIFTS FROM YOUR PARENTS AS WELL.
USE THEM WISELY.
IF YOU DON'T WISH TO TELL ME THE REASON YOU LEFT THE VILLAGE...
...AND BECAME A BOUNTY HUNTER, THAT'S FINE.
YOU'RE WELCOME BACK ANY TIME, AND YOU CAN ALWAYS DEPEND ON ME.

THANKS, CHIEF.

BY THE WAY, ABOUT THOSE RAINBOW PEARLS YOU MENTIONED...
I MAY HAVE SOME USEFUL INFOR-MATION.
IT'S THE LEAST I CAN DO.
YOU'VE HEARD OF THE RAINBOW PEARLS?!
I KNOW SOME-ONE WHO KNOWS SOMEONE...
THEY TOLD ME...

...TO SEND YOU TO THEM...
...ONCE THE THREE OF YOU WERE REUNITED.
KIIII KIIII
I SEE.
THANKS FOR YOUR HARD WORK!
POOF

DID THE SHIKIGAMI COME BEARING GOOD NEWS?
YES!
THE THREE PRINCESSES ARE TOGETHER AT LAST.

THEY'LL BE ARRIVING IN A FEW DAYS.

WE CAN FINALLY SAY FAREWELL TO THIS MOUNTAIN.

WHAT A RELIEF!

THAT MEANS ...

...IN A FEW DAYS WE CAN STOP FEEDING **THESE FREE-LOADERS!**

NOM NOM

HOW DARE YOU! WE'RE HERE TO HELP!

RIGHT? SAY SOME-THING, YAWA-RAGI!

Journey 5:
Barrier

YASHAHIME
PRINCESS HALF-DEMON

A SWORD FOR TOWA... HM...
HOW ABOUT THIS ONE?
HIIRAGIDANJO OUGIGAYATSU, RULER OF KANTO, RECEIVED IT AS A GIFT FROM THE ASHIKAGA SHOGUNATE.
BEHOLD THE FEAR-SOME BLADE KIKUJU-MONJI!
SHING

EXCEPT THAT IT'S A FAKE. AND BROKEN.
NOT ONLY IS THIS...
SHK
...NOT A FEARSOME BLADE, IT DOESN'T EVEN FUNCTION AS A SWORD!

YOU'RE THINKING LIKE AN AMATEUR.

IT'S A REPRODUCTION, BUT A GOOD ONE.
IT CONDUCTS DEMON ENERGY. THE MISSING BLADE MAKES IT LIGHTER.
IT'S PERFECT FOR YOU! YOU CAN USE IT TO CHANNEL YOUR DEMON ENERGY INSTEAD OF FIGHTING WITH A PHYSICAL BLADE.

IS SHE SERIOUS?
YES. YOU CAN PRACTICE FOCUSING YOUR ENERGY TO SPRING FROM THE HILT.
IT'S A GOOD BEGINNER'S WEAPON.
IN BATTLE, YOU CAN ATTACK DEMONS WITH A BLADE OF DEMON ENERGY AND STRIKE HUMANS WITH THE SHEATH.
LIKE A CLUB?!

WE FOUND THIS ON THE DEMON WE KILLED...
THAT MEANS IT DIDN'T DO A VERY GOOD JOB OF PROTECTING ITS **FORMER** OWNER, DID IT?
I'M NOT SURE I WANT TO USE A DEAD PERSON'S SWORD.

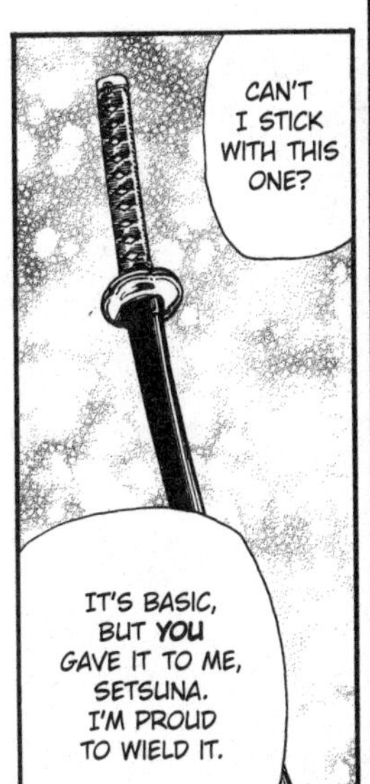
CAN'T I STICK WITH THIS ONE?
IT'S BASIC, BUT **YOU** GAVE IT TO ME, SETSUNA. I'M PROUD TO WIELD IT.

IF THAT'S YOUR CHOICE, I WON'T ARGUE WITH YOU.
BUT **THAT** SWORD CAME FROM THE MAN THE THREE-EYED CENTIPEDE WAS DINING ON.
OH.
GUESS I'LL TRY KIKUJU-MONJI.
TOSS
KLANK

CAN I GET A DEMON-SLAYING OUTFIT LIKE THE ONE YOU TWO HAVE?
YOU MEAN THE OUTER GARB AND BREAST-PLATE?
YEAH. YOU LOOK LIKE NINJA!
MY WHITE SUIT IS GONNA STAIN AND WRINKLE.
TRUE.

I LIKE YOUR CLOTHES.
YOU LOOK GOOD IN THEM.
BUT YOUR ROBE OF THE FIRE-RAT FIXES ITSELF BY MAGIC!
I'LL NEED A DRY CLEANER, A WASHING MACHINE, DETERGENT, FABRIC SOFTENER, DRYER SHEETS, AND AN IRON!
I HAVE NO IDEA WHAT YOU JUST SAID.
I CAN TEACH YOU HOW WE WASH OUR CLOTHES.
WASN'T THAT SUIT...
...CHOSEN SPECIALLY FOR YOU?
I HAVE MY MOM'S SPIRITUAL SENSITIVITY. I CAN FEEL THE LOVE AND CARE IMBUED IN IT.
!
IT'S NO MAGIC GARMENT ...
...BUT IT CAME FROM SOMEONE WHO WISHED TO PROTECT YOU.

THAT'S RIGHT...
EVEN IN THIS ERA, MY SUIT CONNECTS ME TO MY FAMILY BACK HOME.

MEI!
WHAT DO YOU THINK, SIS?
IT'S NOT MY STYLE, BUT IT'LL LOOK GREAT ON YOU!
IT'S EASY TO MOVE IN... WHITE REPELS DEMONS...
IT'S NOT ARMOR, BUT STILL!
HUF HUF
TRY IT ON... JUST FOR A SECOND... PLEASE?!
IT CAME FROM MEI!

THANKS, MEI. I'LL TRY TO KEEP IT CLEAN.
BUT MAYBE NEXT TIME YOU COULD GET ME A SWEATSUIT OR SOMETHING...

SL
ASH
VMMMMMM

AFTER ALL THAT COMPLAINING, YOU'VE REALLY TAKEN TO IT!
YOUR DEMON-ENERGY BLADE IS SHARPER ALREADY!
HEH HEH ...
YOU WERE RIGHT. IT'S EASY TO HANDLE, AND I CAN SEE THE ENERGY I'M PRO-JECTING.

I'M STARTING TO GET THE HANG OF IT.
AT THIS RATE...
...I'LL BE ABLE TO DEFEAT ANY DEMON!!

OF COURSE. YOU HAVE TALENT.
AND YOU'RE MY TWIN.

THE DREAM BUTTER-FLY...

IF I'D BEEN STRONGER...

...THEY COULD'VE GROWN UP TOGETHER.

WHOOPS!
FORGOT I HAD AN ALARM SET ON MY PHONE.
DOODOO DEE DEEDEE

!!
DOODOO DOOO DEEDEE DEEE
YIPE!!
PIP
HUH?

VWWWP
W-WHAT...
...WAS THAT INFERNAL SOUND?!
VWP
SOME SORT OF CURSE?!
NO, NO! IT'S JUST... UM...

"OBVIOUSLY, YOU CAN'T MAKE PHONE CALLS IN THE FEUDAL ERA."
"NO SATELLITES, NO INTERNET, NO GPS."
Campus
How to Conquer The Feudal Era
(5)
SOTA HIGURASHI
"BUT A SMARTPHONE STILL HAS PLENTY OF USEFUL TOOLS—CLOCK, CAMERA, FLASHLIGHT, ETC."

*Excerpt from Sota's Notes

"I'VE DOWNLOADED SOME APPS THAT MIGHT BE USEFUL, LIKE DICTIONARIES, ONTO AN OLD PHONE."

"YOU CAN KEEP IT CHARGED WITH A PORTABLE SOLAR BATTERY CHARGER."

"THE DIGITAL COMPASS USES GEOMAGNETIC SENSORS, SO IT SHOULD STILL WORK IN THE PAST."

"COMBINE THAT WITH A STEP COUNTER AND YOU HAVE BASIC NAVIGATION."

PAPA SOTA, WHAT ARE YOU DOING?

READ TO ME!

SKRATCH SKRATCH SKRATCH

Baboooo

BE-PAL TOP 100 OUTDOOR ESSENTIALS

SHARIHIME

IT'S JUST THAT...
I DIDN'T HAVE TIME TO PREP BEFORE I CAME HERE. THANK GOODNESS FOR PAPA SOTA.
...ALL THE MUSIC HE DOWNLOADED...
...IS SUPER-OLD DAD MUSIC! DON'T JUDGE ME, OKAY?!
I HAVE NO IDEA WHAT YOU'RE TALKING ABOUT.
SO DON'T WORRY.
?
?

ANYWAY, LET'S BREAK FOR LUNCH.
WE'VE GOT RICE BALLS FROM THE VILLAGE AND...
... THIS.

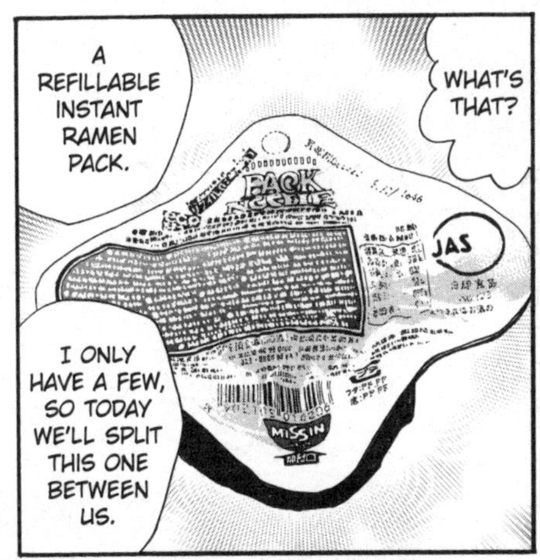
WHAT'S THAT?
A REFILLABLE INSTANT RAMEN PACK.
I ONLY HAVE A FEW, SO TODAY WE'LL SPLIT THIS ONE BETWEEN US.
JAS
MISSIN

RIP

BLUP
BLUP

FWAAAA

EAT UP!
SLURP
OH!
EH?
FLIT
OH, WOW! SO GOOD!

IF I'M READING THE STEP COUNTER RIGHT...
...WE'RE ALMOST THERE.
WE'RE MAKING **INHUMANLY** FAST TIME. WHOO HOO!
TRUTH BE TOLD, WE COULD TRAVEL FASTER IF WE WEREN'T DRAGGING **YOU** ALONG.

WE CAN'T GET TOO CONFIDENT IN OUR POWERS.

THERE ARE DANGEROUS DEMONS OUT HERE... AND SOME FORMIDABLE HUMANS TOO.
MIROKU AND SANGO, THE COUPLE WE'RE GOING TO SEE, ARE TWO OF THEM.

THEY WENT ON ADVENTURES WITH AUNT KAGOME, RIGHT?
YES. THEY WERE CLOSE TO **YOUR** PARENTS AS WELL.
TOGETHER THEY DEFEATED MORE THAN THEIR SHARE OF ENEMIES.

HUH...
!!
KSH

SHF
SHF SHF

TWO DEMONS.
I SENSE **THREE** MURDEROUS AURAS... PERHAPS DEMONS IN CAHOOTS WITH A HUMAN...
TOWA, STAND BACK!
SOME-THING'S NOT RIGHT!
NO WAY!
I CAN FIGHT TOO!

ONE OF THEM IS REALLY FAST!
I'VE NEVER SEEN A DEMON MOVE LIKE THIS!!
FWP
AT LEAST THREE TIMES OUR SPEED...

KLA
OOF!
F
WP
NG
KRAK
HUH ?!
GRAB
NNGH !!
VWIP

HEY, YOU!
VMMM
IRON-REAVER!
GR
AB
HOLD ON!
THAT ATTACK RINGS A BELL!
VSHHH
!!

YOU MUST BE THE DAUGHTER OF KAGOME AND THE DOG!
VSHHH

YES.
THAT'S MOROHA.
THIS IS SETSUNA.
SESSHOMARU'S DAUGHTER.
M-MONK...
...MIROKU!!

THAT'S HIM!!
JUST LIKE SETSUNA SAID...
...HE'S INCREDIBLY TOUGH FOR A HUMAN!
THEN YOU MUST BE TOWA.
FSH

THE TWIN...
...WHO WENT MISSING.
HEH

A DEMON ...
... WOMAN?

THAT'S RIGHT.
I'M FROM THE SAME WOLF DE-MON CLAN AS KOGA.
BUT I WAS WHELPED FAR TO THE WEST.

OH!!
ARE YOU ...
... YAWA-RAGI?!

HUH?
YOU TWO KNOW EACH OTHER?
YOU DIDN'T MENTION THAT TO ME.

HAVE YOU FINISHED TESTING THE GIRLS YET?
FWOOOOO
DROOM
EEP
SANGO TOLD ME TO HURRY UP AND FETCH YOU.
SORRY.

WELL, WE HAVE ...
...MUCH TO DISCUSS. BUT LET'S GET YOU SETTLED FIRST.

SORRY FOR THE AMBUSH.

I TRIED TO STOP THEM, BUT YOU CAN'T TELL THESE OLD-TIMERS ANYTHING.

THEY GOT ALL GIDDY ABOUT PUTTING YOU TO THE TEST.
THEY'RE NOSTALGIC FOR THE DAYS WHEN THEY TRAVELED THE LAND WITH YOUR PARENTS.
SHK SHK
NOT TOO SHORT, PLEASE, SANGO.
IN FACT, COULD YOU LAYER IT WITH AN UNDERCUT?
SOME-THING YOUTH-FUL AND FRESH.

I WASN'T GIDDY!
YOU'VE BEEN PACING AND PLOTTING FROM THE MOMENT YOU HEARD THE DOGS' DAUGHTERS WERE COMING.
HAVE NOT!
TWITCH TWITCH

WE DIDN'T STAND A CHANCE.
I'M ASHAMED.
YOU SHOULD BE!

IF YOU CAN'T TAKE US IN A FIGHT...
...YOU WON'T LAST A MINUTE OUTSIDE THE BARRIER!
IF YOU'RE SO WORRIED, ACCOMPANY THEM.
I CAN'T.
I NEED TO LOOK AFTER MY PACK.

BARRIER...?
WHAT ARE THEY TALKING ABOUT?
LET'S BEGIN AT THE BEGINNING.
IT STARTED THREE YEARS AGO...

MOROHA AND SETSUNA HAD RETURNED, BUT THEIR PARENTS WERE NOWHERE TO BE FOUND. AS WE WERE WONDERING WHAT HAD BECOME OF THEM...
MASTER!
CAN YOU COME WITH ME?
...HACHI SOUGHT ME OUT.

I STUMBLED UPON HIM AS I WAS PASSING BY.
HE DIDN'T WANT ANYONE TO KNOW.
THIS WAY.
!
IT'S...
...JAKEN!
ARGH...
MASTER SESSHO-MARU...
I SEE YOUR MOTHER BECKONING ME...

THE WOUND LOOKS INFECTED.

HE WAS BURNED BY A POISONOUS FLAME EIGHT YEARS AGO.

THE INJURY IS SPREADING ...

I DON'T KNOW WHAT RITES TO PERFORM AT A DEMON'S DEATHBED.

INSTEAD OF PLANNING HIS FUNERAL, WHY NOT TRY **SAVING** HIM?

EIGHT YEARS AGO...

THAT'S AROUND THE TIME SETSUNA AND MOROHA RETURNED.

I KNOW OF SOMEONE SKILLED AT HEALING DEMONS.

PLEASE GO AND FETCH THIS HEALER.

MY MASTER ADVISES THE PATIENT TO TAKE IT EASY.

HE WILL NOT **FULLY** RECOVER FOR SEVERAL YEARS.

HEALED BY A HUMAN... HOW EMBARRASSING.

BUT THANK YOU, UM...

...MONK WHO IS FRIENDS WITH INUYASHA!

TWITCH TWITCH

IS HE WELL ENOUGH FOR ME TO SLAP HIM?

YES.

I'LL BE GOING NOW.

THANK YOU SO MUCH FOR YOUR HELP.

PLEASE GIVE MY REGARDS TO YOUR MASTER.

I SHALL.

BOW

FINE.
BUT I MUST WARN YOU, I HAVE LITTLE TO OFFER.
SIGH
YOU KNOW MASTER SESSHOMARU NEVER TELLS ME ANYTHING. I MEAN... HE'S VERY RESERVED.
HE'S BEING HONEST FOR ONCE.
I THINK I CAN TRUST HIM.
SHORTLY AFTER MY MASTER'S DAUGHTERS...
...WERE BORN...
JAKEN...

I AM JOURNEY-ING TO THE WESTERN LANDS.
I WON'T RETURN FOR SOME TIME.
WHAT?!
DOES THIS MEAN...
...YOU'RE TAKING YOUR RIGHTFUL SEAT AT THE HEAD OF DEMONKIND...
...IN YOUR FATHER'S PLACE?!
OH, HOW I'VE LONGED FOR THIS MOMENTOUS DAY!
YOUR DESTINY IS TO RULE AS THE KING OF ALL DEMONS ACROSS THIS LAND OF THE SUN...
...BUT INSTEAD YOU'VE BEEN CHASING YOUR BROTHER AROUND OR, TO USE THE VERNACULAR, **JUST HANGING OUT.** FRANKLY, I WAS ON MY LAST NERVE!

ASSEMBLE THE TROOPS-
SILENCE.
SQWISH
OOF!
YOU WILL REMAIN HERE.
I LEAVE YOU WITH THIS.
WHAT IS IT?
IT CONTAINS POWERFUL DEMON ENERGY.
KYIIIII
WHEN I HOLD IT, I CAN FEEL ITS POWER FLOWING THROUGH ME!
THE RAIN-BOW PEARL.
SUCH BAUBLES OCCASIONALLY FORM WITHIN DEMONS. ITS PROLONGED CONTACT WITH ITS HOST IS WHAT CAUSES IT TO GLOW.
THE POWER OF THE DEMON WHO HOLDS THE PEARL HARMONIZES WITH THE POWER OF THE DEMON WITHIN WHOM IT FORMED.

THEN YOU SHOULD WIELD IT, MASTER SESSHO-MARU!
HMPH.
YOU THINK I HAVE NEED OF SUCH A TOY?
THERE IS NO PATH DENIED TO ME...
...AND NOTHING I CAN'T ALREADY PROTECT!
...
...?
MASTER ...?

YOU WILL DEFEND THIS HOUSE...
...UNTIL THE HALF-DEMON GIRLS ARRIVE.
HUH? HAS RIN... I MEAN, THE MADAM...
...DECIDED TO LIVE HERE INSTEAD OF WITH INUYASHA'S FAMILY?
NO.
RIN WILL NOT BE COMING.
AND FORGET ABOUT MY BROTHER AND HIS WIFE.
YOUR ONLY TASK IS TO PROTECT THIS PLACE.
IF ANYTHING UNTOWARD SHOULD OCCUR...
FWAASH

NOT SO FAST!
THE CHILDREN WILL DIE HERE...
...AS MASTER ZERO COMMANDS.
MASTER SESSHOMARU PREDICTED THIS!!
THAT'S WHY HE GAVE ME THE PEARL!

BURN TO ASH, MINOR DEMON!!
HYA HA HA!!
BO
OF
HMPH!!
WHA...?
I'VE DIED ONCE BEFORE.
I CAN'T BE REVIVED AGAIN.
H-HOW?!
I REFUSE TO DIE AT THE HAND OF ANYONE BUT MY MASTER!

IT CAN'T BE!
HIS FLAME IS STRONGER THAN MINE...
OH NO!!
GYA
WHOOOOOM
AAAH!!

DOOOOM

UGH ... WHAT A FOOL I AM.

NEVER UNDER-ESTIMATE A DEMON DRIVEN BY DESPERA-TION.

HYOOOO
KTK KTK
KTK

HA!
MWA HA HA!!
I MADE THEM PAY!!
WAHAHAHA HAHA
fsssh
KOFF... KOFF...
KRRH

BUT CHAPER-ONE...
WE'VE LOST TOWA.
GLOOM
HM.
YES. THAT IS...
...A SHAME.
BUT MASTER SAID...
IF WORSE COMES TO WORST...
...AND THE DEFENSES AROUND THIS HOUSE FALL... WE MUST LEAVE.
I'VE PREPARED ANOTHER BARRIER AT THE BORDER.
TRIGGER THAT BARRIER AND IT WILL REPEL DEMONS FROM BOTH THE EAST AND THE WEST.
YES, MASTER, BUT...
...FOR HOW LONG?
UNTIL THE CHILDREN ARE OLD ENOUGH TO LEAVE ON THEIR OWN.

IF YOU LOSE ONE OF THEM, SO BE IT.
IT IS THE TRIAL OF GO-OKU.
A DAUGHTER OF MINE MUST BE ABLE TO CLIMB FROM THE DEPTHS ON HER OWN.

GO-OKU?

WHAT'S THAT?

GO AS IN GO-YU, OR **COURAGE**.

IT'S A TEST OF YOUR METTLE.

IT KIND OF SOUNDS LIKE... HE KNEW I WAS GOING TO GET SEPARATED FROM THE OTHERS.

INDEED.

I BELIEVE EVERYTHING THUS FAR HAS TRANSPIRED JUST AS SESSHOMARU FORESAW.

WHICH MEANS HE'S BEHIND WHATEVER HAPPENED TO THE DOG AND KAGOME!
WE DON'T KNOW THAT, KOGA.
EVEN IF YOU'RE RIGHT, HE MUST HAVE HAD HIS REASONS.

SESSHO-MARU SAVED MY BROTHER.
HE FORGAVE ME AS WELL.
I CHOOSE TO TRUST HIM.

...

HA!
I DON'T KNOW ABOUT HUMANS, BUT...

...THE WOLF DEMON CLAN DOESN'T JUMP TO OBEY COM-MANDS.
WE PUT OUR LIVES ON THE LINE FOR FAMILY AND FRIENDS.
WHEN IT COMES TO A CHILD, THAT GOES **DOUBLE**.
HOW CAN YOU CARE ABOUT THAT GO-GO-WHAT-EVER...

... COMPARED TO POOR KAGOME NOT BEING ABLE TO REAR HER OWN PUP?!

GAH!!

YOU CAN ALL JOIN MY PACK! BE WOLVES!

I'LL FILL YOUR STOMACHS WITH RAW MEAT!!

MEAT?

WE'RE NOT PUPS!

EVEN IF WE **ARE** DOG DEMONS!!

I WASN'T EXPECTING THIS...

WOLVES ARE DEVOTED TO THEIR PUPS.

SO THIS JAKEN WAS MR. SHAPPY, THE CHAPERONE ...
WHERE IS HE NOW?

... THANKLESS LITTLE INGRATE?
GONE.

...!!

I SEE...

HE PASSED AWAY AFTER ALL...

NOPE.

HE DUMPED HIS DUTIES ONTO US AND RAN OFF TO FIND SESSHOMARU.

HUH ?!

MASTER SESSHOMARU NEEDS ME, AND I NEED HIM!

IF I CAN'T TOUCH HIS FUZZY-WUZZY COLLAR REGULARLY, I GO INTO WITHDRAWAL!

DON'T FORGET TO CLOSE THE BARRIER BEHIND ME!!

HE DID LEAVE US WITH **THIS** AT LEAST...
CHAK

THIS IS THE RAINBOW PEARL.
I MAINTAIN THE BARRIER BY MERGING ITS POWERS WITH MINE.
KYIIIIIIIIII
IIII
IT'S NOT **ALL** BAD.
THE HOJO, TAKEDA, AND IMAGAWA FAMILIES PAY US UNDER THE TABLE TO KEEP THE DEMONS OUT.
MIROKU, YOU OLD SCHEMER.
OH!
WHAT'S HAPPEN-ING...?
BRRR
THIS POWER I'M SENSING ...

I FEEL STRANGE ...
BRR
KIND OF HOT AND COLD AT THE SAME TIME...
BRRR

ALL OF YOU? JUST AS I THOUGHT.
WE'VE BEEN STUDYING THE PEARL.

IT EMBODIES DEMON POWER. OVER MANY YEARS, IT GREW INSIDE A DEMON, WHERE IT WAS POLISHED TO PERFECTION.

A PEARL LIKE THIS ONLY FORMS WHEN A CORE OF ENERGY EXPLODES WITHIN A DEMON. WE'RE NOT SURE WHY.

ALL THREE OF YOU HOST RAINBOW PEARLS INSIDE OF YOU.

THOSE PEARLS WITHIN YOU ARE CALLING TO ONE ANOTHER.

IT SEEMS NATURAL TO YOU BECAUSE YOU'RE RELATED BY BLOOD.

AS YOU GROW, YOUR PEARLS WILL BECOME MORE POL-ISHED.
DEMONS ARE BEGINNING TO SENSE THEIR PRESENCE AND POWER.
THE BARRIER KEEPS THEM AWAY FROM US...
...BUT AS SOON AS YOU STEP THROUGH IT, THEY'LL ATTACK IN SWARMS.
WE'VE NOTICED A RISE IN AGGRESSIVE DEMONIC ACTIVITY ON THE OTHER SIDE OF THE BARRIER.
THE BARRIER WAS CREATED TO PROTECT YOU WHEN YOU WERE YOUNG.
BUT NOW YOU MUST LEAVE AND BLAZE YOUR OWN TRAIL.
ARE YOU PREPARED FOR THE BATTLES AHEAD?

THOSE IDIOTS.
CROWING THAT THEY WOULD "VANQUISH" ME.
THEY THOUGHT THEIR SILLY GUNS WOULD HARM ME.
WHAT SORT OF LESSER DEMON DID THEY TAKE ME FOR?

OH.
THIS ONE HAS A GOOD BODY.
THE FACE ISN'T MUCH TO LOOK AT, BUT THE BONES ARE SOLID.
VWP
FWI
OMP

CHOMP
CHOMP
CHOMP
CHOMP
GRIND
KRACK
SNAP
DOES IT TASTE GOOD, FATHER?
IT DOES? I'M SO GLAD!
AH HA HA HA HA
HEY, JAKOTSU-MARU!
HM?
WHAT IS IT, TOTET-SU?
ZSH
ZSH
SNIFF SNIFF
I CAN SMELL IT!
THE SCENT OF A RAINBOW PEARL WAFTING OUR WAY ...

IT'S NOT JUST ONE, EITHER! THREE... MAYBE EVEN FOUR!
AND THEY'RE ABOUT TO COME THROUGH.

BWA HA HA ...
WE MAY EAT THE GIRLS, RIGHT?
AND KEEP THE PEARLS?
GRIK
GRIK
GRIK
MASTER ZERO IS GENER-OUS!
DON'T FORGET, WE'RE **SHARING** THIS MEAL.
YOU CAN HAVE THE MEAT, TOTETSU. BUT LEAVE THE BONES FOR ME.

Journey 6:
Trials and Tribulations
B.A.B.E.

KRAK

KRAKKRAK

RAHHH!
HRRGH!
KRAK KRAK
KRAK KRAK
KRAK
PFFT...

IF YOU'RE STRONG ENOUGH TO BREAK THROUGH A BARRIER...

...WHY DIDN'T YOU DO IT **LAST TIME**?

FOOL! THIS BARRIER IS NOTHING LIKE THE ONE THAT STOPPED US THE OTHER DAY!

YOU KNOW PERFECTLY WELL THAT THE BARRIER OF THE RAINBOW PEARL HAS VANISHED.

THIS FLIMSY THING IS THE WORK OF SOME HUMAN MONK.

GLARE

I DON'T KNOW WHAT IT'S DOING HERE, BUT...
...IT WON'T STOP THE FOUR PERILS OF KIRIN!
FWP
HUH?

TH
OK
NGH!

!
WHOOM
LEAP
SCSSH
THUP

AH, SO YOU'RE ABLE TO DODGE MY ATTACK, ARE YOU?

HAVE I SLOWED DOWN THAT MUCH SINCE I LOST THE SHARD OF THE SHIKON JEWEL?

WOLF DEMON!

I'VE HEARD OF YOU ...

YOU'RE KOGA OF MUSASHI PROVINCE ...

...MERELY A WELL-TRAINED DOG, A PET OF THE HUMANS.
WHAT DID YOU JUST SAY?!

CALM DOWN, KOGA.
HE'S TRYING TO PROVOKE YOU...
SH
SO WHAT?!
THIS PATHETIC LITTLE DEMON HAS NO RIGHT TO TALK TO ME LIKE THAT!
OOM
!
HE'S EVEN FASTER THAN BEFORE!

DMP!
GOOD ...

... RID-DAN-
GSHK
GSHK
GSHK

SHK
SHK
SHK
SHK
WHAT THE...?
BONES ?!
YOU'VE GOT A PEARL IN YOUR LEGS, DON'T YOU?
AND GOOD BONES TOO. HEH HEH!
YOU'LL MAKE A TASTY MEAL, WOLF CUR!

ZV
ZV
ZV
HOLD ON... ARE YOU THE DEMON TOKOTSU?
I HEARD YOU WERE DEAD.
GUESS NOT. FIGHTING YOUR SON'S BATTLES FOR HIM NOW, ARE YOU?
THANKS, FATHER!
DRAG HIM DOWN BY THE LEGS AND SUFFOCATE HIM IN THE SWAMP OF BONES!
UH-OH. TIME TO BEAT A HASTY RETREAT.
HEH HEH HEH! THERE'S NO ESCAPING ME!
ZSH ZSH
ZSH
!
OH NO...
GSHK GSHK

!
HEY, OLD MAN! HAVING TROUBLE?
SHF

GRAB
SO FAST!
WHOA!
VWP
BAM

THE THREE OF THEM OUGHT TO BE ABLE TO GET THINGS UNDER CONTROL.

LURING THE ENEMY WITH A WEAK BARRIER, THEN ATTACKING...

YES...

STILL, THAT ESCALATED FASTER THAN I EXPECTED.

IT'S A STANDARD DEFENSIVE STRATEGY, AND IT WORKS.

BUT KOGA LOST HIS HEAD OVER THE RAINBOW PEARL WE AGREED TO USE AS BAIT.
FLAP FLAP
WHOO HOO!
WHAT'S THIS?!
I CAN MOVE LIKE I USED TO!
I'VE GOTTA RUN LIKE THE WIND! RUN AND KICK!

ANYWAY, THE PLAN IS TO TAKE OUT EVERY DEMON LURED IN BY THE PEARL.

SHF
SHF
ONCE WORD GETS AROUND THAT THERE'LL BE HELL TO PAY FOR ATTACKING THE PRINCESSES OF YASHA...
...THE LESSER DEMONS WILL KNOW TO STAY AWAY FROM YOU ON YOUR JOURNEY WEST.
GIVE...
ZNMMZNMM
ZSH ZSH ZSH
ZNMMZNMM

WE'RE KILLING THESE DEMONS TO SET AN EXAMPLE FOR THE OTHERS. NO MERCY. ARE YOU PREPARED?
YOU BET I AM!
IT'S QUITE THE CROWD...

BUT THE TWO IN THE VANGUARD SEEM TO HAVE BEEN THE STRONGEST.
ONE DOWN, ONE TO...
TWITCH

ARGH!
OWWW!
FWP
!
HE'S...
... COM-PLETELY UN-SCATHED!
HEY, THAT STUNG!
MWF MWF MWF MWF
HOW DARE YOU DIS-FIGURE ...

...MY HANDSOME FACE?

BWA

UH-OH! HE'S EVEN STRONGER THAN BEFORE!
OH NO...
WE HAVE TO FINISH HIM OFF FAST!

SANGO! TOWA!
YOU TWO KEEP UP THE DEFENSE HERE!
FINE, BUT WHERE ARE **YOU** GOING?
SETSUNA AND I WILL TAKE CARE OF THIS DEMON!

BIND!
BWA

HMPH! FOOLS!
YOU THINK SCRAPS OF PAPER CAN STOP ME?
FLAP FLAP
FLAP

!
GRP
GRRP

ARGH!
SKRR

WHA ...?!
CLAP
ARRRGH!
HYOOO
SET-SUNA!
MIRO-KU!

DON'T WORRY ABOUT THOSE TWO.
KOGA AND MOROHA WILL BE BACK SOON.
CHK
A-ARE YOU ALL RIGHT? TALK TO ME!
UNTIL THEN...
SHFF
SKREE!
SHFF SHFF
SHFF
SLVKK
STICK TO THE PLAN! LET'S TAKE OUT THESE DEMONS!
GAH!

I'M GONNA DEVOUR IT!
NAH, I'M GONNA EAT IT!
FIRST COME, FIRST SERVED!
THOOOM
GIMME THE POWER OF THE PEARL!
GET HER BEFORE TOTETSU AND TOKOTSU COME BACK...

AH!
GYA!

YOU DEVOUR ME?
HA HA ...

...SHE WAS A GENTLE SOUL LIKE KAGOME...
...HAVING GROWN UP IN A PEACEFUL WORLD WITHOUT WAR, WANTING FOR NOTHING...
AT LEAST I CAN DO THIS...
... SANGO!

HEH...
ZZ
THERE'S THAT FEELING AGAIN!
ZZ
ZZ

I SHOULD BE SCARED ...
...BUT MY BODY AND MIND ARE TOTALLY FOCUSED. I'M RUNNING HOT AND COLD.

I WAS WRONG.
SHE'S NOT LIKE OTHER GIRLS FROM KAGOME'S WORLD.
VWO
OM
SHE MAY HAVE GROWN UP THERE...
...BUT SHE'S SESSHO-MARU'S DAUGHTER, THROUGH AND THROUGH.

RED DRAGON BLAST!

HEY!
THAT WAS OVER-KILL!
YOUR FLASHY MOVES MAKE ME LOOK BAD!
GSHK
GSHK

I DIDN'T DO IT TO SHOW YOU UP.

I DID IT TO TEACH MOROHA.
HUH?
WATCH AND LEARN. YOU CAN TRY THIS LATER.

I'M SURE YOU'LL MASTER IT.
YOUR IRON-REAVER, SOUL-STEALER HAS ALREADY IMPROVED SINCE I FIRST SHOWED IT TO YOU.

YOU TAUGHT HER IRON-REAVER, SOUL-STEALER?!
YAWARAGI ...
WHAT ABOUT INUYASHA ...?

!
AH!

GIVE ME YOUR LEGS, YOU FILTHY CUR!
I WANT THAT PEARL!

THAT'S ...

...OUR LINE!

GNK

UGH!

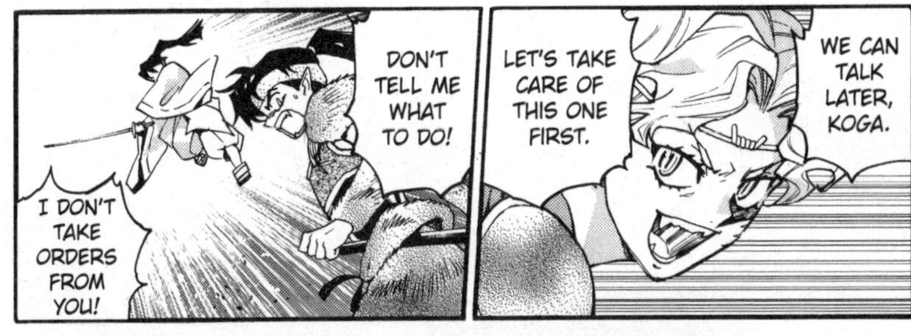

STAND BACK! I'M GONNA FINISH THIS JERK **NOW!**

INSOLENT FEMALE!

I'LL EAT YOU, BONES AND ALL!

ZV ZV ZV

VWP

JUST YOU TRY...

HOLD ON A SEC.

TEP!

?!

THANKS TO YOU...
...I GOT SADDLED WITH 200 RYO OF DEBT!

YEAH, BUT IT WAS GREAT MOTIVATION, WASN'T IT?

BACK THEN, YOU KNEW NOTHING OF THE WORLD. YOU WERE JUST A NAIVE PUP.

YOU HAD DANGEROUS POWERS YOU COULDN'T HANDLE. I COULDN'T JUST STAND BY AND WATCH.

THREE YEARS AGO, SHINANO PROVINCE

ZSH
SURRENDER AND REVEAL YOURSELF, LITTLE GIRL...
SO I MAY KILL YOU!
ZSH
THIS PLACE SHALL BE YOUR GRAVE!
YOUR FATE IS PREOR-DAINED!
HAHAHAHA
BUZZ...
BUZZBUZZBUZZ
FULFILL YOUR DESTINY AND BECOME LORD GAGA'S DINNER!
...
huf
huf

ARGH!
HOW'D I GET INTO THIS MESS?
THUD
THE LOCAL VILLAGERS SAID THEY WERE JUST BUTTERFLY DEMONS...
BUT THESE ARE MOTH DEMONS!
THEY'RE WAY WORSE!
AND THEIR SWARM IS DEVOURING EVERYTHING IN ITS PATH!
MY SWORD AND ARROWS ARE USELESS...
...BUT AT LEAST I STILL HAVE MY DEMONIC CLAWS...
BOFF
I'LL HAVE TO TAKE THEM ON BARE-HANDED!
FORGET IT.
THOSE FLIMSY CLAWS WILL SPLINTER AGAINST THEIR TOUGH HIDES.
!
WHO'S THERE?!

DON'T BE STARTLED.
JUST A FRIENDLY BIG SISTER PASSING BY. ♫
EVER HEAR OF THE WOLF DEMON CLAN?
YOU'RE A WOLF DEMON?
WHAT ARE YOU DOING HERE?
OH, I HAVE MY REASONS.
WHAT ABOUT YOU?
TEP
I'VE GOT MY REASONS TOO, OKAY?
L- LEAVE ME ALONE!
MM- HM... I SEE.
LOOKS LIKE YOU CAME TO PICK A FIGHT...
...WITHOUT KNOWING YOUR ENEMY WELL ENOUGH TO REALIZE YOU DON'T STAND A CHANCE.

GUESS I'LL LEAVE YOU TO GET SLAUGHTERED THEN.
YOU'LL DIE FOR NOTHING, CRUSHED LIKE A BUG...
...AND GOBBLED UP BY THIS SWARM HERE.
HEY!
YOU'LL NEVER SEE YOUR PARENTS AGAIN...
...OR SAVE YOUR FRIENDS.
AND YOU WON'T EVER FIND REDEMPTION.
!
H-HOW DO YOU KNOW ABOUT...?
SNIFFL
COME, NOW...
IF YOU GO INTO BATTLE, YOU MUST ALWAYS BE PREPARED TO DIE.
I JUST ...
... WANTED TO...

... DEFEAT THE BUTTERFLY DEMON...
...TO BREAK SETSUNA'S CURSE.
BUT... I CAN'T.
... YOU'RE WEAK.
WEAK AND COCKY. THAT'S A RECIPE FOR TROUBLE.
IF YOU WANT TO ACCOMPLISH ANYTHING...
...YOU NEED TO BE STRONG YET HUMBLE.
I CAN TRAIN YOU.
REALLY ?!

GHGHGH
GNSSH!
BZT
BZZZZ
GHGH!
BZTBZTBZT
...!
EH?
ZSH
THERE'S
A GOOD
GIRL!
IT
APPEARS
YOU'VE
ACCEPTED
YOUR
FATE.
HEH
HEH
HEH
...
I HEAR
YOU'VE
DEVOURED
A LOT OF
DEMONS AND
HUMANS IN
YOUR TIME.
ARE YOU
PREPARED TO
HAVE YOUR
FEELERS
RIPPED OFF
YOUR UGLY
HEAD?!

SILENCE! HUMANS AND DEMONS ALIKE ARE MY FOOD!
I PREY ON WHAT-EVER I WISH!
CHHK
WHAT THE-?!
THAT'S ARMOR OF THE IRON-RAT.
THE ENCHANT-MENT ON IT WILL REPEL ANY ATTACK-BUT JUST ONCE.

BEWARE, THOUGH... ONCE YOU PUT IT ON, YOU'LL NEVER BE ABLE TO TAKE IT OFF.
IT WILL SHRINK BY INCHES, MONTH BY MONTH... UNTIL IT CRUSHES YOU.
THE FIRE-RAT DEMONS CAN FASHION YOU A KEY TO REMOVE THE ARMOR-BUT IT WILL COST YOU.

I COULD ASK MY FRIENDS TO LOAN YOU THE MONEY IF YOU LIKE...
THEY'RE IN THE DEMON-BOUNTY BUSINESS. YOU COULD WORK FOR THEM UNTIL YOU REPAY YOUR DEBT.
YOU WANT ME TO BECOME... **A BOUNTY HUNTER?!**
WHY NOT? IT'S THE FASTEST WAY TO HONE YOUR SKILLS.

NOT TO MEN-TION...
...YOUR CLAWS.
THEY'RE WEAK. YOU HAVE YET TO LEARN HOW TO CHANNEL YOUR POWER INTO YOUR FINGERTIPS.

DON'T BE TIMID. CONCENTRATE. IMAGINE YOU'RE POURING YOUR LIFE FORCE INTO YOUR CLAWS.
VW
OO
OOM!
YOU'LL FEEL THE
FERENCE.

SHA
HERE'S A MOVE UNIQUE TO THE DOG TRIBE!
IRON-REAVER, SOUL-STEALER!
SHHH
GYAAAH!

BOOF

GHGHGH ...

BUGGING OUT

L-LORD ...

... GAGA!

CHF

ROUGE ?!
EVEN IF I WORE MAKEUP, THIS ISN'T THE TIME–

THAT'S NOT ORDINARY ROUGE. IT'S A WEAPON.
IZAYOI'S ROUGE.
I'VE BEEN KEEPING IT SAFE FOR YOU.

HUH? WHERE'D YOU GET THIS...?
!!

FWOOO
MOROHA!
OOO

YOU CAN DO IT.
YOU CAN FIND YOUR WAY TO US.
FWO
YOU HAVE THE POWER!
AFTER ALL, YOU'RE OUR...
WHAT THE...?
VOICES?!
THIS IS THE **REAL** REASON I CAME TO THIS LAND.
I'VE WAITED EIGHT YEARS TO GIVE THIS TO YOU.
YAWARAGI... WHAT ARE YOU...?

PUT THIS ON AND YOU WILL BECOME...
... BENIYASHA, DESTROYER OF NATIONS!

TURN BLOOD-RED AND VANQUISH YOUR ENEMIES!
VWOO

OWWW!
GY
AHHH
CURSE YOU!
I'LL KILL YOU!

HUH?

GRRF!
GRAAH!

WHAT THE–?!
HE INHALED ALL THE ENERGY I UNLEASHED ON HIM?!

HYOOOOOO
NNGH!
COULD IT BE ...?
I CAN'T BELIEVE IT! THIS IS THE POWER OF...
...A WIND TUNNEL!
HE HAS A WIND TUNNEL DOWN HIS GULLET!

Journey 7: Lifting the Barrier

YASHAHIME
— PRINCESS HALF-DEMON —

GHOOOOO
BWAAAAAH!!
GTNK
GTNK
GTNK
GTNK
TH-
THAT'S
A...
GTNK

...A WIND TUNNEL!
HE'S GOT A WIND TUNNEL DOWN HIS GULLET!

A... WHAT?
A CURSE THAT CREATES A BLACK HOLE INSIDE YOU.
IT CAN BE WIELDED AS A WEAPON THAT DEVOURS EVERYTHING IN ITS PATH!
ONCE YOU'RE DRAWN INSIDE IT, THERE'S NO ESCAPE...
HOW-EVER...
GWOOOOO

HEY, PIGGY!
A LITTLE FRIENDLY ADVICE!
THE WIND TUNNEL IS CERTAIN DOOM!

EVERY TIME YOU USE IT, IT CONSUMES A LITTLE MORE OF YOU!
IN THE END...
!
TUP

HMPH.
YOU KNOW A LOT FOR A HUMAN.
HAWHAWHAW
BUT I ALREADY KNOW THIS POWER IS A DOUBLE-EDGED SWORD.

FWASH
THAT'S WHY...
...I LIKE IT!

I SACRIFICE MYSELF TO VANQUISH MY ENEMIES! MUTUALLY ASSURED DESTRUCTION!
AND WHAT POWER!
MWAHAHA HA HA HA HA HA
AWE-INSPIRING, RIGHT? JEALOUS?

GTINK
HUH ?!
"JEAL-OUS"?!
YOU'VE GOT TO BE KIDDING ME.
YOU HAVE NO IDEA HOW BADLY I LONGED TO BE RID OF THAT CURSE.
THOOM

URGH!
IT HELPED THAT YOU'RE STUPID.
JWP
SHUT
HEY! YOU TRICKED ME! YOU GOT ME TALKING SO YOU COULD JUMP ON ME AND CLOSE THE TUNNEL!
NAGINATA DEMON TECHNIQUE ...
SWING

...SUZAKU AMBUSH!

VWOOSH
TP
FWMM
ARGH!
KRRSHH

DID WE GET HIM?!
NO, THE IMPACT WAS CUT IN HALF.
I SHUT HIS MOUTH, BUT HE INHALED THROUGH HIS NOSE.

YOU WON'T ...
...GET AWAY WITH THIS!
THOOM

DRAT!
EVEN WITHOUT THE WIND TUNNEL, HE'S A TOUGH BRUTE.
THIS IS GOING TO BE HARDER THAN I THOUGHT.

I'D NEVER WANT MY CURSE BACK.
I WANT TO LIVE AND DIE AS AN ORDINARY MAN.

BUT IF...
...I STILL HAD THE POWER OF THE WIND TUNNEL...
...WOULD INUYASHA HAVE TRUSTED ME ENOUGH TO TAKE ME WITH HIM?

IF I STILL HAD ALL THAT POWER IN MY RIGHT HAND...
...WOULD WE BE TOGETHER NOW?

HEY!

BABOOM

WHAT'S THIS?!

LOOKS LIKE YOU COULD USE A LITTLE HELP.
IN THAT CASE...
TEP
!
...YOU'D BETTER NOT WASTE TIME...
...BAR-RAGING ME WITH QUES-TIONS...
GRIN
...OR LECTURING ME ABOUT LEAVING THE VILLAGE.
THE SMOKE ISN'T VERY HARMFUL TO HUMANS...
...BUT IF THE WIND SHIFTS, YOU'D BETTER PUT ON THESE GAS MASKS.
KOHAKU!
CHIEF!
PSHT
A DEMON SLAYER?!
THIS POISON IS NOTHING TO US!
I'LL EAT YOU AND LICK THE PLATE CLEAN!

OH.
TOSS

BOOOM!
GAH!

WHAT ARE YOU DOING HERE, KOHAKU?
THIS IS NO PLACE FOR THE VILLAGE CHIEF!
IF SOMETHING WERE TO HAPPEN TO YOU, WHO WOULD PROTECT YOUR PEOPLE?
AND... I'M GETTING LECTURED ANYWAY.

I KNOW YOU MEAN TO BE HELPFUL...
...BUT YOU STILL BEHAVE AS IF YOU'VE GOT A **DEATH WISH.**
I THOUGHT I TAUGHT YOU TO SET THE PAIN OF YOUR PAST ASIDE AND GROW UP!

BELIEVE ME, I'M TRYING.
SPEAKING OF THE PAST...
...IT APPEARS THIS THUG'S WIND TUNNEL HAS STIRRED UP SOME OLD FEELINGS IN YOU TOO.

HMPH.
GRIN

WELL, THE STRUGGLE TO ABANDON WORLDLY CONCERNS IS PART AND PARCEL OF THE CHALLENGE OF BEING HUMAN.

BESIDES, THE LADIES LOVE MY RECKLESS STREAK!

YOU DON'T SAY?

I'VE STILL GOT A LOT TO LEARN ABOUT ADULTHOOD, IT SEEMS.

BAM!

SO HOW SHALL WE ROAST THIS BEAST?
I'M OUT OF SMOKE BOMBS.
HM... HE'S TOO STURDY TO TAKE OUT BEFORE THE SMOKE CLEARS.
HEY! KEEP AWAY FROM THAT WIND TUNNEL!

SEND ME IN!
AREN'T WIND TUNNELS VULNERABLE TO POISON?

!
SETSUNA, YOU DON'T MEAN...

I DO.
RELEASE THE POWER IN ME...
...THAT YOU SEALED AWAY WHEN I WAS A CHILD!
THUK
YANK

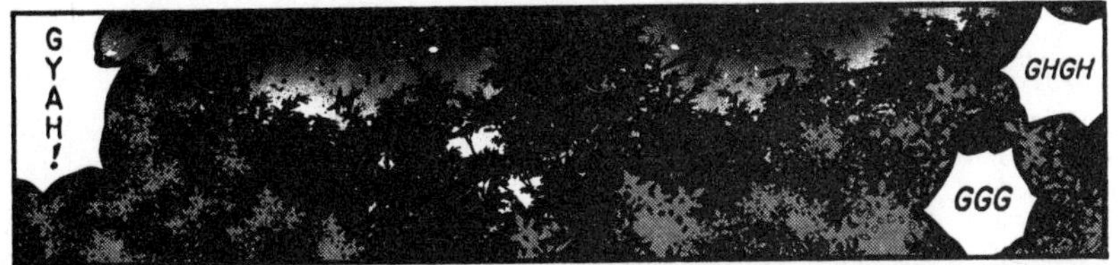

ARGH...
SL
B
ASH
SHHH
AGH!

DRAT!
THERE ARE MORE DEMONS HERE THAN I THOUGHT!
AND TOWA...

THAT LOOK ON HER FACE IS TROUBLING.
BZZT
SHE OUGHT TO BE EXHAUSTED, BUT SHE KEEPS GROWING **STRONGER.**
HEH...
SHE SEEMS TO BE ABSORBING POWER FROM THE DEMONS AS SHE DEFEATS THEM.
THAT MUST BE HER SPECIAL GIFT!
HEH HEH HEH...

BUT SHE'S ONLY **HALF-DEMON.** THERE MUST BE LIMITS TO WHAT SHE CAN HANDLE.
WHEN SHE CROSSES THAT THRESH-OLD, WHAT WILL HAPPEN TO HER?
GYA
GYA
WILL SHE DIE? OR TURN INTO A FULL-FLEDGED DEMON AND LOSE HER HUMANITY?

I NEED TO GIVE HER A CHANCE TO REST...
...BUT THERE'S NO TIME!
WHAT CAN I DO?

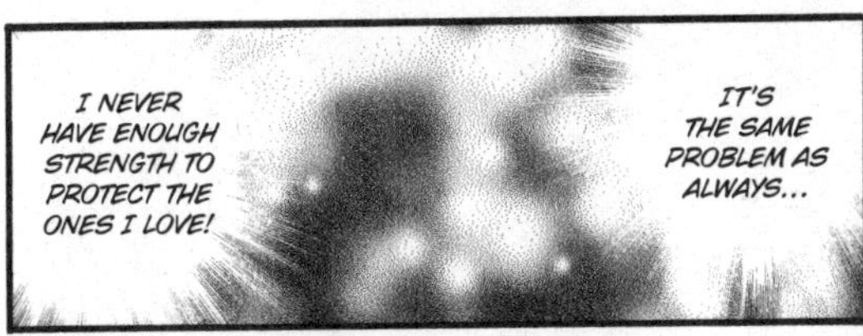

IT'S THE SAME PROBLEM AS ALWAYS...
I NEVER HAVE ENOUGH STRENGTH TO PROTECT THE ONES I LOVE!

WHY DO YOU HESITATE, SANGO?
HOW CAN YOU BE SO UNSURE OF YOURSELF AND...
HUH?

...CLAIM TO BE MY MASTER?
ZB
!
AWANG!
HOW DID YOU GET HERE?
HIRAI-KOTSU?!

HEE HEE!
WE TAGGED ALONG WITH UNCLE HOKUTO. ♫
USE HIRAI-KOTSU, MOTHER!
IT'S BEEN NAGGING ME TO RETURN TO YOUR SERVICE.
VWOOSH

...BESTOW STRENGTH AND COURAGE UPON ME...
...MY TRUSTED PARTNER IN BATTLE!
WHOOSH
WHP
COME ON!
WE CAN'T LET ANY DEMONS GET THROUGH!
DASH
GOT IT, MOTHER!

DISPEL!
FWP
FWP
SLCH
SLCH
SLCH
AHHHH!!

BOOM!

RRRRP
GRAAAH!

ZSSHH
SQWEEK
KYaaa

I CAN ALWAYS COUNT ON YOU KIDS IN A PINCH...
KEEP THE ENEMY AT BAY!
YOU'RE A GREAT HELP!

THAT'S A RELIEF. WE THOUGHT YOU'D YELL AT US FOR SHOWING UP HERE.

IF YOU HAD, I'D HAVE SAID IT WAS ALL HISUI'S IDEA.

TOWA, TAKE A BREAK!
YOU SHOULDN'T PUSH YOURSELF SO–
?!
TOWA ...?

...
SOME-THING'S ...
... COMING ...

ZSHH
SZZZZZ

BOFF
BOFF
BOFF
BOFF
KYAA!
KYAAA!

THE RAINBOW PEARL!
FWOOOOM
AND THE HALF-DEMON BRAT...
I'LL BURN THEM ALL TO A CRISP!
IT'S HOMURA.
WHAT'S HE DOING?
YOU DON'T BELONG HERE!
THAT'S OUR PREY!
YOU USED TO STRUT AROUND CALLING YOURSELF THE GOD OF THE MOUNTAIN...
HEEE HEE HEE HEE
...BUT THEN YOUR FLAMES BACKFIRED ON YOU! WHAT A FAILURE!
THEY SAY EVEN A KAPPA WATER DEMON CAN DROWN IN A FLOOD!
HAHAHAHAHAHA
SHUT...

...UP!
GYAH!
AHHHH!!
!
ARGHH!
GYAHH!

ZZZHHH

W-WHAT IS THAT THING?!
THAT WAS SOME ATTACK!
IF IT HITS US, WE'RE CHAR-COAL!
BURN...
HA HA HA HA HA...
EVERY-THING CAN BURN!

THE PEARL AND THE BRAT!
DEMONS AND HUMANS ALiKE!
I DON'T CARE ABOUT MASTER ZERO'S ORDERS!

HEY! YOU'RE ...
...ONE OF THOSE DEMONS WHO ATTACKED THE MANSION!

"IN HASTE I COM-MAND THEE ACCORDING TO SACRED LAW!"
CLASP
"RELEASE THE SEAL UPON THIS GIRL. LET HER DEMON BLOOD INFUSE HER SOUL!"
KLAWW

AAAAAAAH!!
VWSH

AHHH!!

WHOOSH

IS THAT...
...THE BLOOD SWORD?

WHEN SETSUNA WAS YOUNG, SHE FEARED HER GROWING POWERS.
SHE TRAINED WITH YOU TO LEARN ALTERNATE FORMS OF DEFENSE...
...AND REQUESTED THAT I SEAL OFF THE POWER OF HER DEMON BLOOD.
HOW-EVER...

NOW...
...I COME INTO MY OWN!
IT'S MY HEARTFELT DESIRE TO SAFEGUARD OTHERS...
...AND BE HERE FOR...
...FIND MY PARENTS...
...MY SISTER AND MY FRIENDS!
ARE YOU TRYING TO ATTACK MY WIND TUNNEL?!
NICE TRY, BUT YOU'LL HAVE TO GET THROUGH MY JAWS AND FANGS FIRST!

FOR THEM, I'M WILLING TO USE EVERY-THING AT MY DISPOSAL!
I'LL LEARN TO MASTER THE POWER IN MY BLOOD!
GRASH
FSHHHHHHH
!
THAT'S ...

FZZZZZ
...POISON CLAW!
ZZZZ
KRAK
NO ...
I'M BURNING UP!
KOFF...
KRAK KRAK
...THE WIND TUNNEL... COLLAPSING INSIDE ME...
IT'S IMPLODING!
SETSUNA!
GET AWAY FROM THERE! YOU'LL GET SUCKED IN TOO!

VWIP
GRAB ON!
VSH
KYAH...
KYAAAA!!

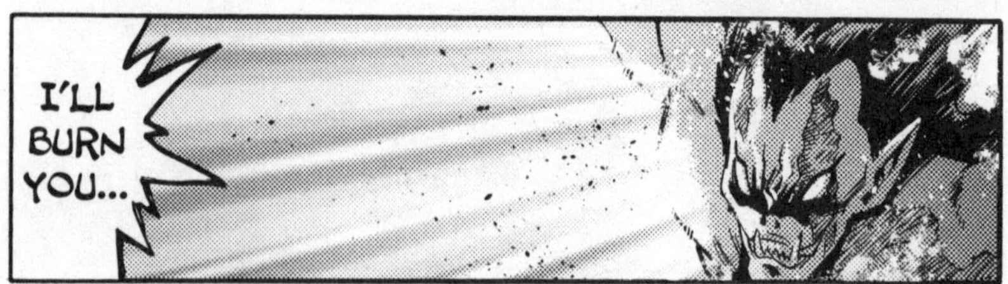

...TO ASHES!
BOF
SHE'S CHAN-NELING ALL HER DEMONIC ENERGY INTO HER SWORD!
THAT BLUE GLOW...
IT LOOKS JUST LIKE...

...
SESSHO-
MARU'S
ATTACK!

AZURE DRAGON WAVE!

AH...
...HA...
AHHH!

D
RMMMMMMM
SHING
KRRKL KRRKL
OOM
!

WHAT WAS THAT?!
TWO HUGE EXPLOSIONS ...
!
DAD!
VO
OM
WHAT ?!
NGH!

DAD?!

D- D...

... DAD!

KRAK KRAK

GSSHH

KRAK SNAP

SNAPESHH
KRAK KRAK KRAK

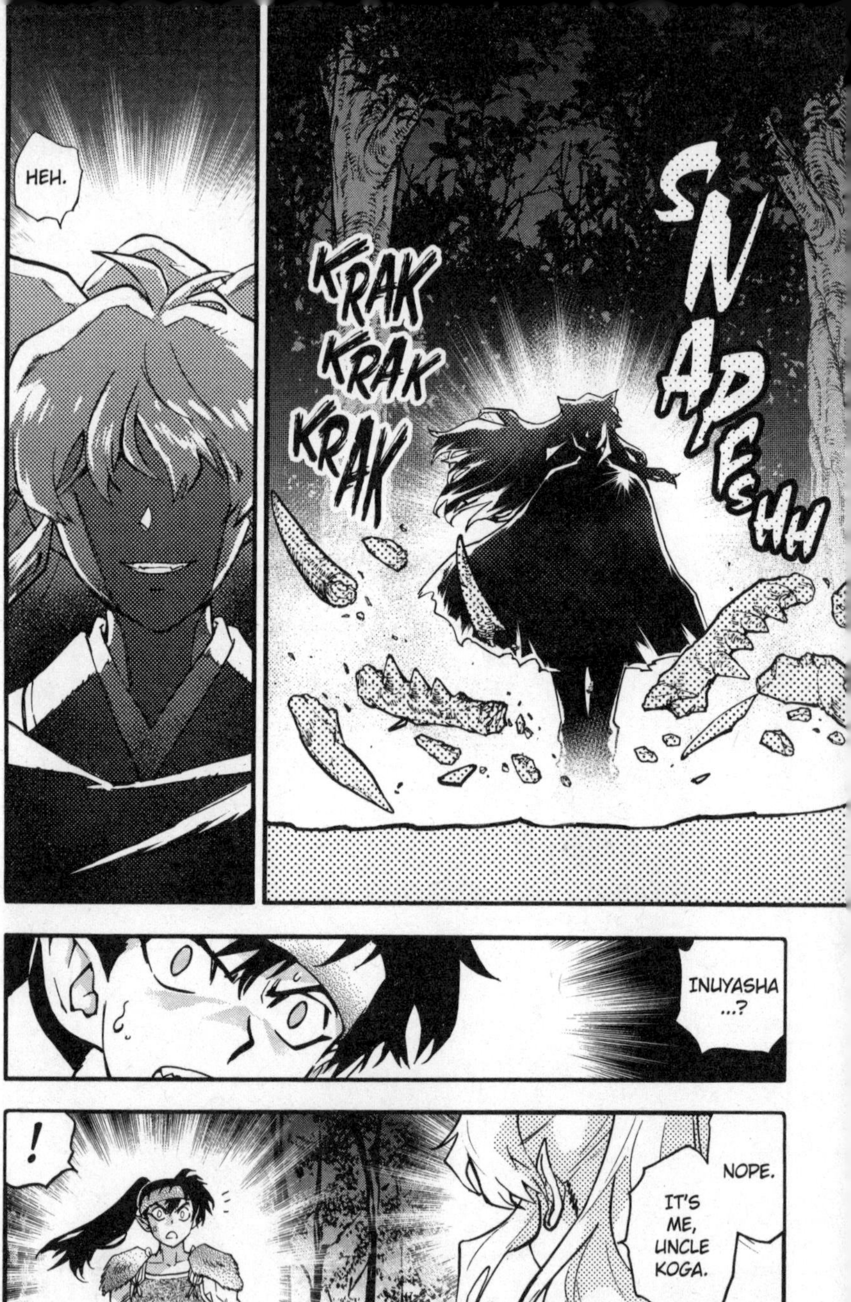

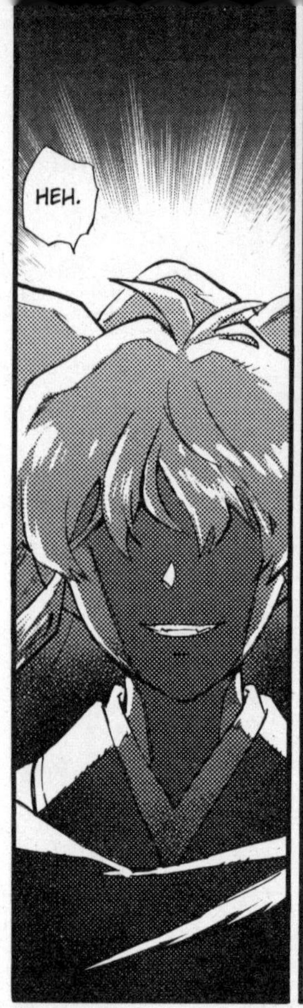
HEH.

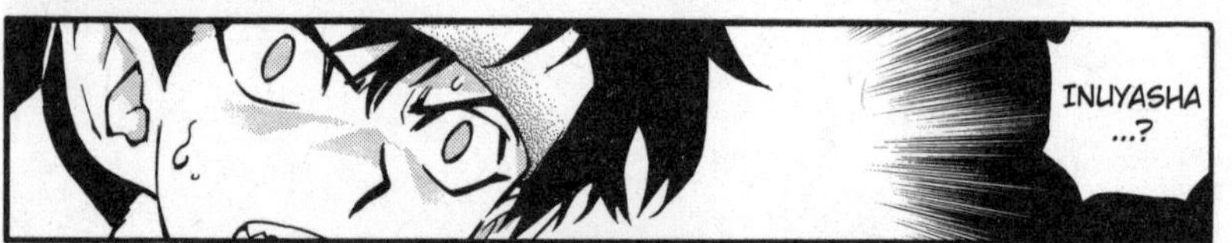
INUYASHA ...?

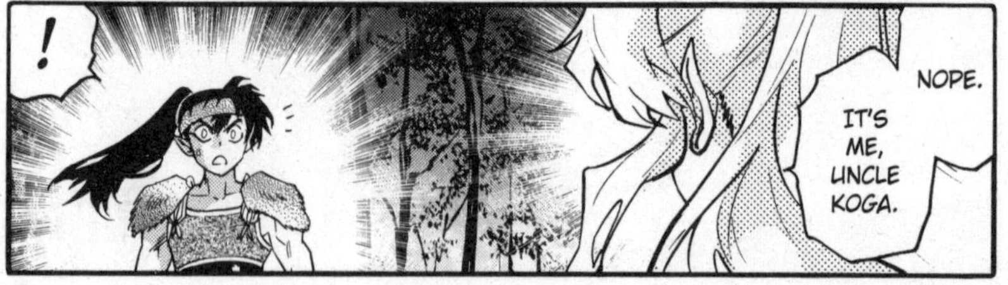
NOPE.
IT'S ME, UNCLE KOGA.
!

I TOOK CARE OF THE BONY OLD DUDE.
ALL THAT'S LEFT IS THAT GOOFY-LOOKING GEEZER IN FRONT OF ME.
LET'S FINISH THIS!
MOROHA?!
YOU LOOK... UH...
HEE HEE HEE!
I'M AT MAXIMUM POWER NOW...
...GOOD, RIGHT?
UHH...
WA
HUH?
HHH
THUD
HEY!
ZSH
!

SHOOM
YOU KILLED MY FA-THER!
I'LL SUCK YOUR BONES DRY AND CRUNCH THEM TO DUST!

HEH.
YOU FINALLY FELL FOR IT...
SMIRK
DOOM
SHAAAA

SHOOM SHOOM
!
SHOOM
MY SWORD IS JUST FOR SHOW.
I NEEDED YOU TO SLOW DOWN SO I COULD GET A CLEAN SHOT.
YOU LEAPT RIGHT INTO MY TRAP.
WHAT ...?!

NO! WE TWO OF THE FOUR PERILS...

FSHHH

...FATHER AND SON...

FSHH FSHH

...CANNOT BE DEFEATED BY THE LIKES OF YOU...

THIS IS MY **REAL** WEAPON...

GORAISHI!

...BUT YOU'VE BEEN FELLED BY A PRECIOUS TREASURE OF THE WOLF DEMON CLAN.

IT'S NOT INFUSED WITH THE PROTECTION OF MY ANCESTORS ANYMORE...

HMPH. YOU OUGHTA BE **HONORED.**

FSSHHHH

WHAT'S WRONG WITH HER?
SO, UM...
FSHHHH

SHE'S FINE. LET HER REST.
ZSH
SHE BURNED THROUGH ALL HER ENERGY, THAT'S ALL.
YAWA-RAGI!
WHAT DID YOU DO TO HER?!

I RELEASED ALL HER DEMON POWER.
AS A MERE QUARTER-DEMON, THERE WILL BE TIMES WHEN SHE NEEDS **ALL HER POWER AT ONCE.**

IZAYOI'S ROUGE IS INFUSED WITH THE PROTECTION OF HER PARENTS.
A CERTAIN SOMEONE ASKED ME TO GIVE IT TO HER.

COME TO THINK OF IT, AREN'T YOU THE ONE...
...WHO TOLD ME ABOUT INUYASHA AND HIS PUP IN THE FIRST PLACE?
YAWARAGI ...
...WHO **ARE** YOU?

WHEN WE FIRST MET, I BOUGHT YOUR STORY...
YOU SAID YOU WERE THE LAST SURVIVOR OF A WOLF DEMON CLAN DEFEATED BY A TYRANNICAL DEMON.
THAT'S A COMMON ENOUGH TALE AMONG OUR KIND.
YOU BROKE BREAD WITH MY TRIBE AND WON OUR TRUST.
YOU WERE A GOOD COMPANION ON THE HUNT.
BUT YOUR SCENT...
...WAS ALWAYS SOME-HOW... OFF.

MY SCENT ...?
YOU'RE DEFINITELY A WOLF DEMON, BUT YOU DON'T HAVE THE RIGHT **SPIRIT**.
I DON'T SENSE ANY VITAL ENERGY IN YOU.

I'VE BEEN WAITING FOR YOU TO COME CLEAN, BUT TIME'S UP!
TELL ME THE TRUTH OR I'LL...
...SLAY YOU AS YOU STAND BEFORE ME.

OH, ALL RIGHT.
VP
YOU'RE KIND, KOGA.
FSSS
A GOOD WOLF.
!

WHOOSH
THIS DEMONIC ENERGY...!
ARE YOU...?
FWP
THOOM

SZZZZ
HEY!
THE PEARL!

THIS IS GOODBYE, KOGA.
GIVE MY REGARDS ...
...TO MOROHA AND THE REST OF THE PACK.
FSSSS
SSSH
SS
I'M FORTUNATE TO HAVE MET THEM.

YAWA-
RAGI!
FS
S
S
S
S
SO YOU
WERE...
...
DEAD ALL
ALONG...
S
S
H

DID YOU HEAR?
THE DEMONS WHO WENT AFTER THE PEARL...
PSST PSST
PSST
THEY WERE WIPED OUT!

REALLY?!

THE PRINCESSES OF YASHA ARE FORMIDABLE INDEED!

I SEE... I SEE...

HOMURA AND TWO OF THE FOUR PERILS WERE DEFEATED.
MURMUR
I THOUGHT THE PEARL WAS INSIDE A MERE HALF-DEMON GIRL.
MURMUR
MURMUR

THAT'S RIGHT.
BUT IT SEEMS WE UNDER-ESTIMATED HER.

ALL THE DEMONS ARE DISCUSSING IT IN HUSHED VOICES...
THEY ARE PRINCESSES OF YASHA... YASHAHIME.
...
BEWARE, BEWARE!
KOGA!

THE ONLY DEMONS WHO WOULD INTERFERE WITH THE GIRLS' JOURNEY NOW WILL BE STUPID...
...OR SERIOUS ENEMIES.

HOW'S THE DEMON GOSSIP GOING?
JUST AS YOU PLANNED.
RUMORS ARE SPREADING LIKE WILDFIRE.
GOOD.
THEN WE CAN SEND THEM ON THEIR WAY WHEN THEY WAKE UP.
THEY'VE PASSED OUR TESTS.
TO BE HONEST, I'M SURPRISED.

THESE GIRLS ARE MORE POWERFUL THAN WE THOUGHT.

THEY SHOULD BE ABLE TO FACE ANYTHING THEY MEET ON THE ROAD.

ZZZ

SHNRF...

ZZZZ

YOU IDIOT! I ALREADY KNEW THAT!

I MEAN, THINK WHO THEIR **PARENTS** ARE!

WHAT'S WRONG, MISS?
...
SHYAAAA
HEH. IT SEEMS YAWARAGI DID WELL.
THAT MEANS...
...OUR WISH IS ABOUT TO COME TRUE.
...?
JUST LEAVE IT TO RIKU...
...MISS RION!
MMF.
HNGH.
To be continued...

BONUS INTERVIEW WITH RUMIKO TAKAHASHI AND TAKASHI SHIINA

The long-awaited interview with Rumiko Takahashi, legendary creator of *Inuyasha*, and Takashi Shiina, who pens *Yashahime*, continues!

How was it reading Takahashi's manga for the first time?

Shiina: I read *Urusei Yatsura* in middle school when it was first serialized, and I thought, "This is the start of something big!" It was set in a fantasy manga world, but the characters were modeled after real people. I was surprised that they seemed like they were really there. I thought, "If you can make *these* characters seem real, imagine the potential for other manga!" That's how Takahashi's work became the catalyst for me to enter the manga world. That's how great an impact she made on me.

"Imagine the potential."

What do you mean, "it seemed like they were really there"?

Shiina: The characters in manga up till then would express themselves directly and pretty much mean what they said. That was the norm, especially with kids' manga. But when Takahashi came onto the scene, her characters' speech had subtext.

Previously, characters lacked dimension and nuance. Her portrayal of multi-dimensional characters was a leap forward. Plus, her stories were slapstick comedies. Those two elements in one manga really surprised me.

Takahashi, were you conscious of this innovation when drawing your manga?

Takahashi: I didn't think about it at all. I've always just wanted to have fun drawing manga and hoped that my audience would laugh along. I love shonen manga, and I was reading a lot of that at the time. What Shiina is describing is something I learned from a variety of sources. I think when I began working professionally, I'd been stockpiling inspiration from manga and novels. Those were the elements I wanted to put into my work, and I guess everything just clicked into place.

Lum and Ataru from *Urusei Yatsura*, the manga that inspired Shiina.

Takahashi, what was the first manga by Shiina that you read?

Takahashi: I read his four-panel joke manga *Shiina Department Store*. When the series began in *Sunday*, I thought to myself, "It looks so effortless. How can it be so good when he isn't a veteran manga artist?" I wondered what he had worked on before to get to that level. When *Ghost Sweeper Mikami* began, I really enjoyed its momentum. Shiina's work still has that energy. I can tell he puts a lot of thought into his characters. His manga are such a pleasure to read. Those were my first impressions of him.

"I wondered what he had worked on before."

From the short story "Pocket Knight," included in *Shiina Department Store*, one of Shiina's first works.

Do you think it was the near-professional quality of his work that led you to believe that his first series was effortless?

Takahashi: That's right. It just appeared one day in *Sunday* without any fanfare. I remember reading it uncritically. He was so young yet so professional.

Shiina: (LOL).

Takahashi herself appeared in *Ghost Sweeper Mikami*. How did that happen?

Shiina: Well, I asked her if I could put her in the manga. (LOL) I wanted to have a 1970s vibe when I flashed back to Mikami's boss's younger days—like a time-travel story. At that time, Narita International Airport was still being built, and the Shinjuku skyscrapers didn't exist. But those details alone would have been boring, so I wanted to add in some of *Sunday*'s history. I told Takahashi that I wanted to include a scene about the moment *Urusei Yatsura* was born. I asked her permission, and then I went ahead with it. She got mad at me afterwards though. (LOL)

Takahashi: He asked me for permission, and I said, "Sure." I let him take care of the rest. (LOL). I think it's another interesting feature of Shiina's storytelling style.

Ghost Sweeper Mikami: the story behind the legendary scene.

Thank you both very much!

Hmooo
IF I HAVE TO CHANGE MY DEBUT MANGA TITLE KATTE NA YATSURA (SELFISH GUY) ...
...I'M GOING TO MAKE THE MAIN CHARACTER SUPER LUCKY!

Trivia: *Ghost Sweeper Mikami* is a work of fiction, but some of the characters are based on real people.

Rumiko Takahashi appears from *Ghost Sweeper Mikami* vol. 37 on. It's totally her!

Takashi Shiina

Story and Art

Takashi Shiina debuted in 1989 with *Shiina Department Store*. His first ongoing series, *Ghost Sweeper Mikami Gokuraku Daisakusen!!* (Ghost Sweeper Mikami: The Great Paradise Battle!!), was a huge hit. His manga *Psychic Squad* ran until July 2021 in the magazine *Weekly Shonen Sunday*. His series *Yashahime* is serialized in *Shonen Sunday Super*.

Rumiko Takahashi

Main Character Design

The spotlight on Rumiko Takahashi's career began in 1978 when she won an honorable mention in Shogakukan's prestigious New Comic Artist Contest for *Those Selfish Aliens*. Later that same year, her boy-meets-alien comedy series *Urusei Yatsura* was serialized in *Weekly Shonen Sunday*. Takahashi followed up the success of her debut series with one blockbuster hit after another—*Maison Ikkoku* ran from 1980 to 1987, *Ranma 1/2* from 1987 to 1996, and *Inuyasha* from 1996 to 2008. Her recent notable work includes *Rin-ne* and *Mao*.

Takahashi was inducted into the Will Eisner Comic Awards Hall of Fame in 2018. She won the prestigious Shogakukan Manga Award twice in her career, once for *Urusei Yatsura* in 1981 and the second time for *Inuyasha* in 2002. A majority of the Takahashi canon has been adapted into other media, such as anime, live-action TV series, and film.

Yashahime: Half-Demon Princess is set in the world of Takahashi's *Inuyasha* and continues the adventures of the original characters as well as their descendants.

Shonen Sunday Edition

STORY AND ART BY TAKASHI SHIINA
MAIN CHARACTER DESIGN BY RUMIKO TAKAHASHI
SCRIPT COOPERATION BY KATSUYUKI SUMISAWA

Translation ◆ **Junko Goda**
English Adaptation ◆ **Shaenon K. Garrity**
Touch-Up Art & Lettering ◆ **James Gaubatz**
Cover & Interior Design ◆ **Kam Li**
Editor ◆ **Annette Roman**

Original Cover Design: Hitoshi SHIRAYAMA + Bay Bridge Studio

Printed in the U.S.A.

Published by VIZ Media, LLC
P.O. Box 77010
San Francisco, CA 94107

10 9 8 7 6 5 4 3 2 1
First printing, December 2022

viz.com

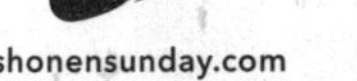

PARENTAL ADVISORY
YASHAHIME: PRINCESS HALF-DEMON is rated T for Teen and is recommended for ages 13 and up. This volume contains fantasy violence.

In keeping with the original Japanese comic format, this book reads from right to left—so action, sound effects and word balloons are completely reversed to preserve the orientation of the original artwork.

Check out the diagram shown here to get the hang of things, and then turn to the other side of the book to get started!